2020–2021

THE ENGAGED
CITIZEN

**A SELECTION OF STUDENT WRITING FOR THE UNIVERSITY OF KENTUCKY'S
DEPARTMENT OF WRITING, RHETORIC, AND DIGITAL STUDIES**

The Engaged Citizen

A Selection of Student Writing for the University of Kentucky's
Department of Writing, Rhetoric, and Digital Studies
University of Kentucky
2020–2021

Printed in the United States of America
10 9 8 7 6 5 4 3 2
ISBN: 978-1-61740-894-6

Van-Griner Learning
Cincinnati, Ohio
www.van-griner.com

President: Dreis Van Landuyt
Project Manager: Maria Walterbusch
Customer Care Lead: Lauren Houseworth

Kirkman 894-6 Su20
317228-321920
Copyright © 2021

Table of Contents

Table of Contents

Editor's Introduction

Brittany Sulzener

This year I have had the great pleasure and privilege of editing the *Engaged Citizen*. I am incredibly proud of the students whose work you will find in this textbook. This collection reflects the range of genres, media, and styles represented every semester in the WRD classroom. In these pages and on the companion website, you will find documentaries, podcasts, websites, annotated bibliographies, essays, rhetorical analyses, transcripts, proposals, photo essays, and more.

As in the WRD classroom, these projects cover a diverse range of topics. I am perhaps most proud of these students' efforts to ask important questions about issues facing students on the University of Kentucky's campus, including a documentary that examines food insecurity on campus and the 2019 UK hunger strike, a photo essay about what it is like to be a Hispanic student at the University of Kentucky, and a website exploring how gender and sexual identity impacts students' experiences on campus. This year students explored local campus spaces from White Hall Classroom Building to the Wildcat Pantry, and they looked outward into the Lexington community to consider the impact of local art and social media influencers. These projects tackle issues of racial justice, the false individuality sold by the clothing industry, the stigma associated with majoring in the arts, the race gap that exists in outdoor recreation, and more. In short, this collection of projects represents what is possible when WRD students ask meaningful questions and dedicate themselves to answering those questions with exceptional research and analysis.

I would like to thank these students, both for agreeing to share their projects and for their exceptional work in the WRD classroom. I would also like to thank the instructors who taught these students, helped spark their curiosity, guided them throughout the composition process, nominated their work, and wrote introductions for their projects. Thank you to this year's outstanding group of WRD Mentors—Jannell McConnell Parsons, Emily Handy, Kendall Sewell, and Jillian Winter—for reading, viewing, and listening to all of the submissions and selecting these projects for inclusion. Thank you to Dr. Brian McNely, Dr. Jim Ridolfo, Dr. Jenny Rice, and Dr. Jeff Rice. Without their support, this year's *The Engaged Citizen* would not be possible. I would also like to thank Jason Carr for his tireless efforts to keep everything in the WRD department running smoothly.

Finally, I would like to thank you, the WRD students reading this textbook. *The Engaged Citizen* would not be possible without the contributions of talented and earnest WRD students like you. I hope you will find it helpful, that you will learn something new within its pages, and that you will consider nominating your own work for future editions of *The Engaged Citizen*.

Sincerely,

Brittany Sulzener

Documentaries

The Heart and The Gut—
Food Insecurity at U.K.

Dean Farmer, Melicity Fraley, Alexis Gauger, William
Bodron, Meagan Nye, and Colleen Scott

In March of 2019, students from SSTOP Hunger announced that members
of their organization would be participating in a hunger strike in order to
pressure UK to create a Basic Needs Center. In my WRD 112 course that
semester, the students behind the documentary "The Heart & The Gut—
Food Insecurity at UK" had already collected a significant amount of footage
from interviews with representatives from the university and Aramark, but
they recognized the potential opportunity to document a historic moment
and decided to continue filming.

Dean Farmer, Melicity Fraley, Alexis Gauger, William Bodron, Meagan Nye,
and Colleen Scott were in the right place at the right time, but they also
pursued interviews with students from SSTOP Hunger and made smart
editing choices that affected the tone of the documentary. I love that their
willingness to adapt and shift focus as the situation changed resulted in an
award-winning documentary that provides an in-depth look at the successful
advocacy by STOPP Hunger to create a Basic Needs Center at UK.

—John Barbour

Link to Project

https://wrd.as.uky.edu/engagedcitizen2020

What's Wrong with the Wildcat Pantry

Chloe Kellom

My WRD 111 course asks students to choose a place they can investigate and connect to an issue of local and national importance. For her documentary, Chloe chose to investigate inflated food prices at the Wildcat Pantry, which she adeptly connected to food deserts in her own home city. Chloe's documentary showed a clear passion for her topic as well as an incisive authorial voice, which she continued to sharpen as she revised her video over time. Through these revisions and her passion, she shed light on an issue affecting people here on UK's campus and, indeed, across the country. Chloe's documentary was a highlight of my semester, and I am happy to know that others will now be able to see it and reflect on her findings.

—Brandon West

Link to Project

https://wrd.as.uky.edu/engagedcitizen2020

Influencer Marketing and Credibility

Molly Armstrong, Gracie Elliott, Justine Enright, Olivia Klee, Dalton Morris, Jacob Travelstead

There's so much you can say about social media marketing; its ubiquity can be overwhelming, not just for us as consumers, but for those trying to craft a short documentary with a clear and relevant focus. That's what makes "Influencer Marketing and Credibility," the documentary created by Molly Armstrong, Gracie Elliott, Justine Enright, Olivia Klee, Dalton Morris, and Jacob Travelstead in my Fall 2019 WRD 112 course, so brilliant: they expertly focused on the roles of two local social media influencers as examples of the trend, and they utilized voice-over to connect those local stories to the larger issues related to social media marketing. The other thing that makes the documentary so great is the editing. In addition to the professional and consistent voice-over, the documentary expertly weaves together interviews from different perspectives and skillfully incorporates eye-catching visuals and memorable background music. "Influencer Marketing and Credibility" is informative, engaging, and clever.

—John Barbour

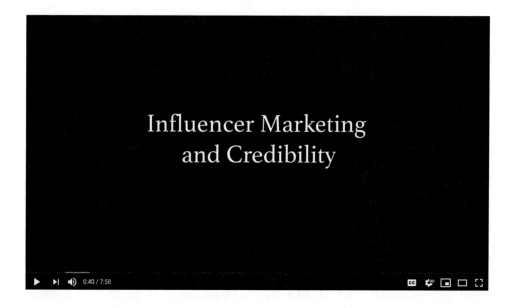

Link to Project

https://wrd.as.uky.edu/engagedcitizen2020

Laundry Room Etiquette

Paige Metcalf

Throughout the Fall 2019 semester, students in my WRD 110 class explored local spaces and human experiences in the community surrounding both the University of Kentucky and Lexington. For the final project of the semester, students were asked to make a video—a public service announcement, specifically—that centered on an issue, tension, or informational need presented by or within the "chosen space" they worked with for all their projects. In "Laundry Room Etiquette," Paige Metcalf uses music, live-action narrative sequences, descriptive text, and an accessible organizational pattern to craft an important, clear-cut message about the Blazer Hall laundry room: "Be responsible and clean when using the laundry room!" Overall, Paige's project is polished, detailed, and a treat to watch, based on the high-quality filming and her effective editing choices. Furthermore, one of the things I appreciated most about Paige's video was the strong and consistent demonstration of audience-awareness that is detectable throughout the narrative. I am extremely proud of Paige's work, not only in this charming PSA video, but also throughout the entire WRD 110 semester.

—Jillian Winter

Link to Project

https://wrd.as.uky.edu/engagedcitizen2020

Essays

Fitting In and Standing Out: How the Clothing Industry Sells False Individuality

Abigail Carney

I love reading student work that stimulates my own thinking on the subject, and Abby's essay does exactly that in its exploration of how the clothing company UNIQLO uses narratives of identity and individuality to sell its products. Beyond its technical excellence, what makes this paper so special is that it transcends the typical confines of a rhetorical analysis to consider some of the larger implications of its claims, like in its discussion of our "culture of consumerism" in which "commodities seem to have transferred into something greater" leading "people [to] try to buy their way to being themselves." Overall, Abby's work is genuinely insightful, and a wonderful example of what students can achieve when they aim to dig deeply into their subject matter.

—Zach Griffith

Fitting In and Standing Out: How the Clothing Industry Sells False Individuality

Confusion sells. Encouraging consumers to be both unique and stylish, interesting, but not counter-cultural and to stand out, but in the right way, advertising specializes in the construction of unattainable ideals and campaigns in which diametrically opposed ideas meld into one seemingly cohesive argument that appeals to the masses. By playing on the most pervasive human desires, the desire to fit in, and the desire for individuality, clothing companies in particular are able to suspend society in limbo between the two. This, naturally, leaves consumers feeling unfulfilled as they try to satisfy the standards handed to them. Clothing certainly can be used as a means to both blend in and stand out; at its best, it is used as an artful expression of the wearer—at its most basic it is simply a means to cover our bodies. Most, however, seem to fall between the two as they grapple with what to wear to both blend in and make a statement. UNIQLO, a small but mainstream clothing brand, seems to capitalize on this dichotomy. They promise clothing that provides a tailored, individualized experience that fits the buyer's unique needs and sends exactly the message the consumer wants; at the same time, their advertisements seem to cater to the message that outside perception and opinion is what matters most. Through tapping into the individuality narrative as well as the social desire to fit in, companies such as UNIQLO sell clothing as an extension and fulfillment of their customer's vision for themselves.

UNIQLO's marketing strategy begins, simply, with the company name. In titling themselves so unapologetically and boldly, they exploit the cultural narrative of individuality and uniqueness. The brand name acts as an umbrella over the entire shopping and purchasing experience and, subliminally or not, leads consumers to feel as though they are aligning themselves with a "unique" brand that will make them stand out. Interestingly enough, the clothing they sell is generally neutral, basic and trendy. Such stark division between the products themselves and the promises made by the name "UNIQLO" makes it almost seem as though they are "hiding behind a smile," delivering bland while promising interesting.

Following this theme, the launch of UNIQLO's "Lifewear" campaign introduced a new slogan: "Why do you get dressed? We'll keep asking. That's the science of Lifewear." This slogan asks the consumer what they want in their clothing and insinuates that UNIQLO will provide according to their individual demands. One particular advertisement released within the Lifewear campaign, a commercial created for the knitwear line, patently demonstrates this tactic. In the production, a narrator directs several questions at the viewer, beginning by asking, "What can a sweater say about you?" and ending by inquiring what kind of person the viewer wants to be: "So who do you want to be today? An extra, or the lead?" In between, the narrator asks the viewer similar questions, seemingly searching for their personal aspirations. These questions paratactically build to form a complete and clear message of how the consumer should interpret their company: they are a brand that will align with the customer's vision, rather than asking them to align with theirs. They drive the message home with the pledge that their knitwear line will fulfill this vision, finally promising that their "premium knitwear [is] made for whoever you want to be." In turn, the intended audience, through this interrogative, second-person diction, is the single, specific viewer who is watching the advertisement rather than a large, general audience.

This viewer-specific and blatant call to individuality and personal expression, however, is incompatible with the imagery displayed in the video itself. Visuals of neutral, simple sweaters, and a cool, slow, and minimalist theme conflict with the verbiage in the narration, as the call to "be yourself" is overwhelmed by the monotonous images on the screen. At one point, the question is posed, "Can you wear the same thing, but feel completely different?" As this question is asked, the camera pans to two women crossing paths while wearing the exact same plain gray sweater. It almost seems as though the company is offering an antithesis to their own argument, conceding that the sweater is nothing special, but because it is a UNIQLO sweater and the wearer is unique, it will showcase the individuality and differentiation described by the narrator. Undoubtedly, the most confusing part of the campaign is the apparent call to individuality, while an obvious ode to conformity dances across the screen. In the advertisement, not only are the two women shown wearing the same thing, but surrounding people are all bland-sweater-clad. It seems as though the only variation between the clothing items is the hue of taupe or gray of the fibers used to create them. Through pitting such opposing ideas against each other, companies leave consumers unsatisfied with any purchase that they make, as it will always lack in one of the two departments. While consumers are often chastised for wanting more every time that they purchase something, this is clearly a result of the discontent created by and for the industry to leave customers in a constant state of wanting. It becomes increasingly clear that the purpose of the entire campaign is to overshadow the nature of the products themselves with the promise of uniqueness, which perpetuates the cultural struggle between conformity and individuality.

Can you wear the same thing but feel completely different?

The UNIQLO advertising campaign, while it does plainly illustrate the dichotomy, is a result of a greater narrative that is coded into society. As consumerism takes over, commodities seem to have transformed into something greater than themselves. UNIQLO, along with many other clothing companies, are trying to sell clothing as individuality, rather than selling the thing for what it is and letting the individual decide what it means to them. In doing so, they perpetuate the concept of "self as project," the persisting idea that each individual is incomplete and in need of constant, unachievable improvement (Cronin 276). Through framing each person's individuality as a goal to be reached, rather than an eminent attribute to be showcased, clothing companies are able to appeal to the intense insecurity created by this notion in promising that their products will lead their customer one step closer to fulfilling themselves and being "whole." This construction is particularly problematic in that rather than recognizing the unique gifts and specializations that each person inherently houses and expanding from them, therefore growing the self, the idea of "self as project" as used in advertising campaigns can be pictured as an endless container to be filled. This leads to the culture of consumerism, wherein people try to buy their way to being themselves in an effort to complete themselves as a person, rather than to express themselves as the distinct individual that they are.

The mixed messages that companies send through advertising speak directly to the difficulties faced by people trying to express themselves while also being told that they aren't themselves without certain items. This divergence can be extremely confusing, and is played on relentlessly by UNIQLO's advertisements. Returning to the knitwear commercial, it is clear that the brand wants the viewer to believe that they have intrinsic singularity. The questions posed make it seem like they care about each consumer's perspective, and the tag line at the end of every Lifewear ad—"… made for whoever you want to be"—reaffirms this assessment. Undeniably, the idea is clear at first; they seem to suggest that they will cater to the viewer's unique life, goals, and desires, and that they recognize the individuality that each person offers. Yet, the content of the questions themselves blurs this message. The opening line, "What can a sweater say about you?" suggests that the sweater is the vessel through which individuality is communicated; therefore, the sweater becomes integral in the process of expressing to the rest of the world that the wearer is unique. It is, rather than an article of clothing, a mouthpiece for the wearer to communicate who they want to be, and a step up on a perpetual staircase to achieved individuality.

Focusing in further, we can begin to comprehend how this narrative can negatively affect individuals' perceptions of themselves. In her essay "From Work to Consumption. Transatlantic Visions of Individuality in Modern Mass Society," Andrea Wirsching describes how "in modern mass societies the construction of selfhood depends ever less on work and ever more on consumption," arguing that in modern consumer culture "it is through consumption that individual identities are constructed and defined." She expands on Karl Marx's phrase, "the fetishism of commodities," explaining that material objects have, as a result of capitalism, extended beyond their use and become mystical in nature. This stretch of meaning can be used to explain how clothing is sold as an idea, rather than a thing. By telling us that what we have is worth more than the work that we actually do, companies are able to capture us into this consumerism and hook us on their brand. In this case, UNIQLO's clothing is individuality in the form of clothing— an extension of the wearer—and therefore has a meaning beyond what it realistically is.

After customers have created an unachievable vision for themselves due to the ingrained idea that they are incomplete, companies attempt to compose a brand image that aligns with the consumer's goals, personality, and outlooks. As published in the findings of a doctoral research project at Fernando Pessoa University in Portugal, companies create a defining brand personality that aligns with their customers in a phenomenon dubbed "self-concept congruence." The study found that, in order to construct a feeling of self-expression within consumerism, brands associate themselves with certain narratives that appeal to and align with their consumer base's interests. This makes the individual feel "seen," like the interaction is personal, and as if the market has narrowed to tailor itself to the individual's pillars—of course, it hasn't. The study categorizes these brand personalities into five sectors: sincerity, excitement, competence, sophistication, and ruggedness. It correctly hypothesized that the subjects involved would adhere to brands in tune with their personality, confirming self-concept congruence and the idea that companies create a world in which buyers feel like they can buy products that they know are mass-produced, but still feel as though they are celebrating their personal values and interests in doing so (Azevedo). This is where UNIQLO's strategy shines; they don't adhere to one category. Instead, they give the illusion of choice. They let the consumer decide, or at least let the consumer think that they are deciding, what vision the company has for them. Therefore, their brand personality is malleable to the desires of every person. In asking who the viewer is rather than telling them what UNIQLO stands for, they allow themselves that opportunity, and it works beautifully in their favor in the context of self-concept congruence and brand personality/consumer alignment.

Unquestionably, advertising is one of the most prevalent and influential components of our society. By playing on powerful human desires, companies bake themselves into the lives of individuals. In turn, those individuals feel as though they cannot live without the things that they have. They become a collage of their things—an aimlessly expanding, moldable result of modern consumerism. Abiding by the rules that the perpetuated narratives lay out for them, they believe that they cannot achieve through their given abilities but instead must turn to commodities to reach their goals and complete themselves. Expectedly, this barrage of things cannot ever fulfill the most innate desire for individuality and unique experience. For this very reason, and knowing that in our society, people will turn to goods for fulfillment, clothing companies such as UNIQLO promise to provide individuality for those who buy their products. They capitalize on the desire for tailored, individual experiences that make their customers feel special. As consumers, it is incredibly important to recognize the sappy truth of individuality: it is intrinsic. It is not something to be bought, sold or otherwise, and each person provides a unique perspective that is wholly separate and individual. In my opinion, it is much more interesting to hear what people have to say, rather than what their sweater has to say about them.

Works Cited

Azevedo, Antonio. "Clothing Branding Strategies: Influence of Brand Personality on Advertising Response." *Journal of Textile and Apparel, Technology and Management,* 2005. *Google Scholar.* researchgate. net/profile/Antonio_Azevedo7/publication/289986521_Clothing_B_ randing_Strategies_Influence_of_B_rand_Personality_on_ Advertising_Response/links/57ea2b8d08aed0a29131a725.pdf. Accessed 6 March 2019.

Cronin, Anne. "Consumerism and Compulsory Individuality: Women, Will, and Potential." *Transformations: Thinking Through Feminism,* 2000, pp.273–277. books.google.com/books?hl=en&lr=&id=6EpmE0 FwQeoC&oi=fnd&pg=PA273&dq=individuality+and+advertising&ot s=kJnGaoZRqW&sig=IsbcyJtK1Z-du1nGjyomFriqzBw#v=onepage&q =individuality%20and%20advertising&f=false.

"UNIQLO | The Science of LifeWear | Knitwear." *Youtube,* uploaded by UNIQLO UK, 15 September 2016. https://www.youtube.com/watch?v= Mn4VlRN0SzI.

Wirsching, Andreas. "From Work to Consumption. Transatlantic Visions of Individuality in Modern Mass Society." *Contemporary European History,* vol. 20, no. 1, Feb. 2011, pp. 1–26. *UK Libraries.* cambridge-org.ezproxy.uky.edu/core/journals/contemporary-european-history/ article/from-work-to-consumption-transatlantic-visions-of-individuality-in-modern-mass-society/988862C8D37865527E23C4CD 35341C62/core-reader.

Understanding the Race Gap in Outdoor Recreation

Claire Hilbrecht

For our WRD 112 rhetorical analysis essay, I asked students to find and analyze a scholarly article through the library database that was related to a final project topic they had already chosen. This required students to have a compelling, controversial, and somehow personally relevant issue chosen early on in the semester; Claire met these requirements and more. Claire took her personal interest in rock climbing and used it to build a fascinating semester-long inquiry into which bodies are and aren't encouraged to access rock climbing. This thoughtful rhetorical analysis essay assesses an article on race and outdoor recreation and serves as a model analysis of argumentative rhetoric as well as a masterful engagement with important ideas in scholarly texts.

—Emily Handy

Understanding the Race Gap in Outdoor Recreation

"Racial Complexities of Outdoor Spaces: An Analysis of African American's Lived Experiences in Outdoor Recreation" is an academic article written by Matthew C. Goodrid that aims to expose and understand the racial disparities in outdoor recreational activities. The exigence for this piece is the lack of racial diversity in outdoor recreational activities. Although racial minorities make up "39.9% of the US population" according to the 2014 Census (US Census Bureau qtd. in Goodrid 11), in 2013, "70% of outdoor recreation participants were Caucasian" (Outdoor Foundation qtd. in Goodrid 11). While it is evident that a racial gap in outdoor recreation exists, its reasons for existing is multifaceted and not fully understood.

This text responds to the narrative of the complex development of the relationship between African Americans in the United States and the natural environment. It attempts to address the problem of racial disparities in outdoor recreational activities by analyzing the historical and contemporary sides of this narrative. The contents of the article show that this is a systematic and institutionalized issue that needs to be addressed. Goodrid gives concrete facts and analyses to enhance his argument while also utilizing the voices of those directly affected by racial exclusion in outdoor pursuits through interviews with African American millennials. Thus, to a large extent, this piece of rhetoric effectively argues its claim that "racial power imbalances exist within the outdoor recreation industry" to its target audience of academics through the rhetorical choices made (Goodrid 5). Due to the extensive length of the article, this rhetorical analysis will be limited to providing a general overview of the rhetorical choices made in the piece as a whole.

The research question that this article attempts to address is: "[Are there] relationships between the sociohistorical development of outdoor recreational spaces, existing environmental habitus and African American lived experiences of outdoor recreation" (Goodrid 14). Goodrid begins the article by providing historical context by delving into African Americans' relationship with the outdoors. He analyzes policy and historical events specific to the African American experience with wilderness, such as slavery in America and the 1964 Wilderness Act, to suggest that "African Americans have a far more complicated union with the natural world compared to European Americans" (Goodrid 30). Additionally, he interviews twelve African American millennials about their lived experiences with outdoor spaces, utilizing direct quotes from the interviewees to conduct a narrative that most accurately guides his research. Through analyzing historical events and environmental policy, as well as through the results of his interviews, Goodrid concludes that outdoor activities are seen by many African Americans as a 'white activity,' and "the low participation rates of African Americans in outdoor recreation is a complicated social phenomena that is connected to multiple facets of oppression" (Goodrid 82). These facets include the "whiteness" that dominates the field of outdoor recreation, a socioeconomic gap that exists between people of color and white people in the United States and the "environmental trauma that African Americans have experienced in outdoor settings throughout American history" (Goodrid 82).

The rhetor is an African American Studies and Sociology researcher from the University of the Pacific, who, through this paper, is defending his thesis regarding the race gap in outdoor recreational activities. Based on the "Acknowledgements" section of this article, it seems that Goodrid's place as a stakeholder in the issue of racial exclusion from outdoor activities lies in the fact that he is a passionate researcher who hopes to understand the complexities of this issue so as to best address it. Goodrid identifies himself as white. As such, he is not directly affected by racial exclusion in outdoor recreational activities. However, as a researcher in the fields of African American Studies and Sociology, his stakes in the issue lie in his academic interests and personal passions.

The text seems to target an audience composed of fellow academics. Goodrid's paper is written as an academic article, with "Review of Literature," "Methodology," "Findings" and "Conclusion" sections. In the body of the article, he cites specific legislation and events that have prevented African Americans from positively connecting with the outdoors in the way that whites have. This, in conjunction with Goodrid's use of advanced language, might make it difficult for the common person to fully comprehend the piece. Additionally, given the context of the text—the article was written for research purposes and is located within an academic online database—one must conclude that the primary target audience is indeed other academics, perhaps in the author's same field of African American Studies and/ or Sociology.

When reviewing the effectiveness of this piece of rhetoric, it is important to understand its constraints. To address a material constraint, the piece is limited in its ability to provide a perfect representation of the relationship between people of color and outdoor recreational activities. It is impossible to interview every person of color on their relationship with outdoor recreational activities; for this reason, the author has limited himself to interviewing twelve people. With this, the people interviewed for this article are all African American millennials. This limits the perspective offered, as an African American's experience with outdoor recreation is different from another person of color's experience, and only a younger generation is represented. Additionally, culturally, race is a sensitive and complex issue, so the article is limited in its ability to fully illustrate the extent of the racial problems that exist in America and how they have affected the outdoor recreation industry. Finally, the piece is limited by its genre. It is a thesis defense paper that is subject to the rules and conventions of academic writing. The author must attempt to remain objective, which affects the rhetorical choices made. For example, the author must maintain a certain level of formality, which may hinder his ability to connect with a wider audience. Instead, he is limited to addressing primarily other academics. This restricts the impact of the piece, as well; while the piece may be effective at articulating its ideas to an academic community, it may not be effective at resolving the wider issue that exists in American society.

The author uses logos to more effectively structure and direct his argument. For example, Goodrid cites specific legislation and historical events to suggest that the current race gap in the outdoor recreation industry has its roots in deeper, more complex issues. He further utilizes logos by developing his article in a chronological and highly orderly manner. In the body of the paper, he first gives historical context to the relationship between African Americans and the natural environment, then references policy that has further negatively affected this relationship and finally shares his results of the interviews conducted with African American millennials. Thus, each piece of evidence builds on and draws from the other, resulting in a cohesive argument.

Similarly, the author uses pathos to appeal to emotion and experience when he interviews twelve African Americans about their experiences in regard to the outdoors and includes direct quotes from the interviewees in the text. He explicitly makes known in the paper that he wishes to make their voices heard, so he decides to include their interview answers directly rather than attempt to paraphrase them and misconstrue the intended meaning of their words. This is a powerful rhetorical device, as it makes the author reliable and draws from the lived experiences of those who are actively being affected by this issue.

Furthermore, the author utilizes ethos to build his credibility. For example, Goodrid's use of interviews appeals to his ethos, as he is made more credible when he takes into account the lived experiences of African Americans who experience this issue first-hand. It helps combat his lack of credibility as a white person attempting to articulate and understand the complexities of the relationship between African Americans and the outdoors. Additionally, his position as a researcher in African-American Studies and Sociology also appeals to his ethos, because one can assume that he has years of experience in and knowledge of these fields. Thus, he is a credible source on a topic that addresses both fields of study.

In addition to these three rhetorical appeals, Goodrid uses several rhetorical devices to effectively argue his claim to his target audience. For example, the author's use of formatting establishes him as a professional researcher who knows how to clearly lay out and articulate his research. He utilizes headings and subheadings to make the contents of the text easy to follow. Additionally, Goodrid chooses to maintain an academic tone throughout the piece, which helps him be well-regarded by his audience of academics. Thus, they are most likely more willing to accept his argument, as it is presented professionally.

Goodrid's use of logos, pathos, ethos, formatting and tone helps him effectively argue to an audience of academics his claim that the race gap in outdoor recreation is due to complex historical and cultural issues. While not an academic, as an outdoor recreationalist myself, I am a stakeholder in this issue in that I hope to be a part of an inclusive outdoor recreation community. Thus, I respond well to this article, viewing it as a step toward making the race gap visible to all those with stakes in this issue—academics, outdoor recreationalists, people of color, etc. The wider outdoor recreation community has begun to notice the lack of racial diversity in outdoor recreational activities. There have been several articles and analyses written in response to this growing issue. While there have been many magazine articles and blogs written about this public issue, it has been more difficult to find academic articles that address the race gap in outdoor recreation. Goodrid's work is a part of this larger conversation, while fulfilling the great need of giving this issue academic credence.

Works Cited

Goodrid, Matthew C. *Racial Complexities of Outdoor Spaces: An Analysis of African American's Lived Experiences in Outdoor Recreation*, University of the Pacific, Ann Arbor, 2018. *ProQuest*, http://ezproxy. uky.edu/login?url=https://search-proquest-com.ezproxy.uky.edu/ docview/2050214873?accountid=11836.

The Rhetorical Analysis of the WWI Poster

Faisal Nadheer Al Balushi, Mian Al Zaabi

In today's political climate, we seem to hear a single message over and over again: Be afraid. Be very afraid. In our Fall 2019 section of WRD 111, my students and I focused on the rhetoric of fear and threat, diving into the language and images that a society under attack uses to describe, prepare for, and respond to a perceived threat. We specifically try to ascertain how the rhetoric of fear can either unite a community or tear people apart. For their midterm project, my students completed the Signs of the Times Rhetorical Analysis Essay, in which they engaged in archival research to find a poster or sign from a time in which the United States was at war or responding to some kind of existential threat. They used their rhetorical analysis skills to determine the purpose behind a sign's message and drew upon their research abilities to place their chosen signs within their proper historical contexts. For their essay, Faisal and Mian chose a poster from World War I in which the U.S. government implores women to purchase war bonds. These talented writers thoughtfully and clearly organized their essay in a way that both highlights their mastery of rhetorical analysis and appeals to a public audience. They thoroughly deconstruct all of the elements of their chosen image and put them into conversation with what was going on when the poster was released. In particular, they deftly assess the poster's reliance on gender politics and the obligation of maternal protection to place their poster within larger conversations about women's roles in a wartime society. Ultimately, Faisal and Mian created a beautifully crafted and engaging piece of public scholarship that probes their readers into asking difficult questions about how we respond to threat and what our obligations are to a country at war.

—Emily Naser-Hall

The Rhetorical Analysis of the WWI Poster

Introduction

A poster is a combination of visual and textual elements aimed to present a particular object or concept. Posters have always been used as a powerful means of promoting a certain idea or product among consumers. Yet, during wartime, they turn into the powerful propaganda tool that encourages people to act in a certain way. This propaganda method is used by all countries; the only thing that differs is their content and purpose. In this paper, an American poster from the period of World War I will be analyzed in terms of its content, context, and visual form to identify its message and delve into that time period, trying to understand the then-society.

The Content of the Poster

In the poster in question, an elderly woman with the arms extended towards the viewer is drawn. Her hair is neatly combed and pinned up with a barrette. In fact, there are few wrinkles on the woman's face, so her age can be guessed primarily from her gray hair. The woman's head is slightly tilted to the side, while her lips are parted, showing a smile. Overall, her face looks rather kind and generous. The woman is dressed in a white blouse and dark skirt, which make up an official style. Behind the woman, there is the flag of the

United States with the inscription "Women! Help America's sons win the war." Hence, it turns out that the she invites American women to financially support the U.S. soldiers by buying the so-called liberty bonds, as it is stated at the bottom of the poster. In the background of the poster, you can see a restless sea, with waves hitting against a rock. The water in the sea is grayish, just like the sky above. On the right, there are small silhouettes of men with weapons and the American flag, moving towards the sea. In addition, it seems like there are dead bodies in the sea, who must be American soldiers. On the left, a boat with a few people is balancing on the wave. Overall, apart from the peaceful woman, the war is demonstrated in the poster.

The poster contains a number of symbolic features, which underscore its main idea and message. Putting an elderly woman in the foreground is the key rhetorical strategy used in the poster under consideration. In any society, the elderly are associated with wisdom and experience. They are highly respected and trusted, because they have gone through many events and world changes. In particular, a smiling elderly woman is likely to win over many people. Looking at the person in the poster, it is quite hard to ignore her request to buy liberty bonds. Her face and extended hands, ready to embrace, make up an image of a reliable, helpful, and sincere person, who can be trusted. In other words, she gives people hope. Furthermore, her official clothing style adds seriousness and importance to the poster. With the flag behind, the woman looks like an embodiment of the U.S., creating the impression that her request to buy liberty bonds is an obligation, supported by the American law. This further reinforces the significance of this liberty bonds program and thus manipulates women, coaxing them into participating in it.

Another essential symbolic element in the poster is the gray sea and sky in a stormy weather. These must stand for the chaos of the war. The gray color in this case is associated with anxiety, disturbance, and restlessness. It shows that the war has been lasting for a long time and that it brings only losses to the American people. Furthermore, the silhouettes of the soldiers and, presumably, dead bodies reinforce the atrocities brought by the war. Consequently, the combined image of the elderly woman and the sea produces a double effect on the viewer. Accordingly, looking at the poster, the latter is likely to conclude that the war is horrible for the nation and that carrying out the smiling woman's request can put an end to the armed conflict. Such a contrast in the atmosphere of the back- and foreground strongly influences the viewer, persuading them to take action.

The Context of the Poster

As for the poster's context, it is easy to understand from the inscriptions. Consequently, there is an essential fact that points out that the image was created during WWI: at the bottom of the poster, the year 1917 is mentioned along with the information about the second liberty loan, which was a hallmark of that historical period in the U.S. This is further supported by the inscription at the top part of the American flag, which addresses primarily women, thus determining the poster's target audience.

Liberty bonds were the U.S. government's financial program aimed at supporting the country's soldiers during WWI. These were sold for at least $50 and were promoted primarily through the posters similar to the one under analysis (Hilt and Rahn). In particular, they depicted the elderly, women, and children, who are typically considered the most vulnerable social groups. Women played the role of the objects of sympathy and stood for justice in such posters. Consequently, the latter was a well-thought-out marketing project, which successfully persuaded people to purchase liberty loans. The image of the woman is definitely powerful in these posters, in particular when accompanied by rather emotional short mottos that determined the thoughts of thousands of the U.S. females (Shover 475-476). Accordingly, the pictures of women were exploited by the government first of all in order to appeal to the whole female population in the country.

The program of liberty bonds was available for both of the genders, but since numerous young men joined the U.S. army, it was more logical to address women, the majority of whom did not fight and had money. In other words, American women played a crucial role for the U.S. propaganda, complying with all the rules and censorship obligations that were relevant at the time. When numerous men left their homes for war, women became the main breadwinners and, correspondingly, the powerful workforce that substantially contributed to the U.S. economy. At the same time, they had to do their household chores and to raise their children. The independence of the American women was gradually increasing as they had to make decisions on their own and to rely primarily on themselves (Litoff and Smith 9). Being self-reliant and earning money on their own made women exemplary citizens, who were perfect for carrying out the state obligations. Left alone at home, women became more empowered and they realized it. In fact, the U.S. government skillfully manipulated this power, reminding women of it through such "call-to-action" posters. In order to get what it wants, the government underscored the importance of women and thus successfully made them purchase liberty bonds, making them believe that they would help their husbands, brothers, etc.

In May 1917, the National Women's Liberty Loan Committee that was a female-only organization was created by Eleanor, Secretary McAdoo's wife and President Wilson's daughter. The organization ardently supported liberty bonds and motivated a number of people to purchase them. The National Women's Liberty Loan Committee collaborated with various female clubs and fraternities, including the Daughters of the American Revolution, the Women's Suffrage Association, the Young Women's Christian Association, and much more. In fact, the organization managed to engage a countless number of women, raising a great sum of money. Furthermore, American priests prayed for the women who bought the bonds every Sunday and disseminated their sermons in the country. For instance, numerous copies of the *Suggestions for Liberty Loan Sermons* handbook were distributed to different states at the time (Hilt and Rahn). In general, it is hardly possible to underestimate the role of women in promoting liberty bonds and subsequently helping the American soldiers at the front.

The Visual Form of the Poster

People usually pay less attention to visual form, considering it only the additional aspect to an image. However, visual effects impact people quicker than any other. Such factors as font, size, and color implicitly affect viewers, evoking certain emotions and thoughts in them, while they do not even realize it.

In the poster that is being analyzed, the text is the main source of content, which is executed in different colors and letter size. Accordingly, the word "women" at the top of the poster is bigger than the others, which means that the creator of the image wanted to draw people's attention to it. Furthermore, the word is painted in yellow, a color associated with sunshine and hope. Hence, women are emphasized as those who can change the situation for the better. Then, the words "help America's sons win the war" are smaller and painted in white. The latter is a neutral color that must be used here to merely convey the request. Interestingly, the words "win the war" are in bold, apparently intended to draw the viewer's attention to them, as they express the desire of millions of Americans. Finally, the text in the bottom is red, with the words "2nd liberty loan" in bold as they carry the key message there. Presumably, the red color, associated with aggression and passion, was used to boost the target audience determination. It is also worth mentioning that all the letters in the poster are capitalized to increase the importance of the message.

Conclusion

Posters, being a powerful means in marketing, prove to be influential during wartime. In fact, due to the combination of an image and text, they turn out to be effective in war propaganda. The image of the elderly woman accompanied by the request to buy liberty bonds proves that posters can make people take certain measures. Indeed, the WWI posters that promoted liberty bonds informed a great number of Americans about the program and, accordingly, motivated them to take part in it. Under the influence of the propaganda, which targeted primarily women, people organized or joined the clubs which supported liberty loans and were mainly female dominated.

As a result, an incredible sum of money was raised for the American troops. Overall, putting an elderly woman asking people to purchase liberty loans did miracles in the American society, skillfully manipulating it by means of content, context, and visual form.

Works Cited

Hilt, Eric, and Wendy M. Rahn. "Turning Citizens into Investors: Promoting Savings with Liberty Bonds During World War I." RSF: *The Russell Sage Foundation Journal of the Social Sciences,* vol. 2, no. 6, 2016, doi:10.7758/rsf.2016.2.6.05.

Litoff, Judy Barrett, and David C. Smith. "American Women in a World at War." *OAH Magazine of History,* vol. 16, no. 3, 2002, pp. 7–12.

Shover, Michele J. "Roles and Images of Women in World War I Propaganda." *Politics & Society,* vol. 5, no. 4, 1975, pp. 469–486., doi:10.1177/003232927500500404.

Porteous, R H. *Help America's Sons Win the War.* 1917, Poster, Edwards and Deutsch Litho. Co., Chicago.

Podcasts

White Hall Audio Essay Podcast

Hailey Petty

Throughout the condensed 2019 summer semester, students in my Freshman Summer Program WRD 110 class explored physical spaces, cultures, and communities within and surrounding the University of Kentucky's campus. In a single week—and grappling with the challenge of working with a less-populated, less-bustling UK campus setting—they created audio essay podcasts to highlight the human experiences that happen in their chosen spaces, drawing upon primary research, such as interviews and personal observations, and soundscapes. In Hailey Petty's podcast, which explores a specific outdoor greenspace near White Hall Classroom Building, she interviewed total strangers to delve deeper into the shifting, changing culture of this social space. One of the things I valued most about Hailey's podcast was how her interviews truly shaped her conclusions about the space. In other words, rather than starting from a foregone conclusion about this seating area's culture and overall atmosphere, Hailey gleaned information from the interviewees before crafting her narration segments and podcast thesis. Additionally, Hailey put a significant amount of revision work into the transcript for this podcast, and it was a pleasure to both hear and read her final efforts.

—Jillian Winter

Link to Project

https://wrd.as.uky.edu/engagedcitizen2020

Bolivar Art Gallery Podcast

Elyssa Gall

Students in my WRD 110 classes are asked to work with and explore local spaces in the greater Lexington community. For the second project of the Fall 2019 semester, each student was tasked with creating an "audio essay podcast" that investigated the culture and human experiences of their chosen space, in order to discern the different possible meanings their space embodies for people. This assignment required students to integrate interview segments, to provide their own narration and reflective commentary, and to weave in location-specific soundscapes. Throughout the semester, Elyssa Gall chose to work with a unique and often overlooked space—the Bolivar Art Gallery, which is located in the University of Kentucky's School of Art and Visual Studies Building. Elyssa's project successfully investigates the atmosphere and cultural experiences that the Bolivar Art Gallery offers, and I was exceedingly impressed by her podcast's organization, descriptive details, and thoughtful narration. Elyssa is a captivating writer and speaker, and her audio essay showcases so many subtle, helpful, and interesting features. From her usage of sound effects to her masterful delivery style, Elyssa effectively encourages her listeners to "come together and wonder together" in the dynamic, diverse, and curiosity-inspiring environment of the Bolivar Art Gallery.

—Jillian Winter

Link to Project

https://wrd.as.uky.edu/engagedcitizen2020

Bolivar Art Gallery Podcast Transcript

Me: Hello everyone and welcome to my podcast. My name is Elyssa Gall and I'm going to be talking today about the Bolivar Art Gallery, one of my favorite spots on University of Kentucky's campus. If you ever get the chance to stop by the Bolivar Art Gallery, for even just 20 minutes, you should. I always go there if I need to get away or get inspired and it is a great place to get immersed in the culture on campus. The culture in the space is very unique because it is always changing, developing, and taking on new forms. You never know what you are going to find when you walk into the Bolivar Art Gallery. In most cases everyone who comes to the gallery has a different experience and is impacted in a different way. Because of this, I interviewed a few different types of people that go to the gallery. I interviewed a UK student who has been to the gallery a handful of times with her friends. And then I interviewed two UK art students who have been to the art gallery many times. By doing this I got to see how their opinions and thoughts about the gallery changed based on their experience.

Something I love about the gallery is that it attracts all types of people and there's no certain "type" of person that goes into the gallery. Also, people react to the gallery in different ways. Some look at the works in silence. [10 second silent soundscape] Some just tilt their head and mumble to themselves. [10 second hmmmm soundscape] And others will chat at a low level about the art pieces, how they feel about them, and contemplate the artists' choices. [10 second chatter soundscape]

I first interviewed Jessica Hallberg, who is not in the school of art but has been to the gallery a few times with her friends. I first asked Jess, what about the Bolivar Art Gallery draws you in?

Jess: Every time I walk in its something new, even if it's the same exhibition I still really enjoy it because even if like it's like the same pieces something different draws me in about them (Hallberg).

Me: What is unique about the Bolivar Art Gallery in comparison to other galleries?

Jess: I think it's interesting because it's oriented towards the students and there is a lot you can learn from going in.

Me: What feeling do you get in the Bolivar Art Gallery?

Jess: I always feel intrigued because I want to see what has changed since the last time I was there.

Me: What kind of people do you usually see in the art gallery?

Jess: There is always a large variety in the gallery because not just art students go there, everyone can go there, and everyone that goes has a different background.

Me: It's great to see how the gallery affects and attracts students who aren't in the visual arts school. It shows how culture in the space is very welcoming to all students and is very diverse. Also, the space brings people together, like Jess said, even students that aren't in the arts feel a connection with the space. Something that I thought was interesting is that Jess mentioned that even though she has not been to the Bolivar Art Gallery that many times she still noticed that it is changing a lot and the people who come to the gallery really get to see what the art culture is like on campus at UK. It really shows how the Bolivar Art Gallery is important to the culture on campus because it brings forth a lot of different ideas that students don't get to see at any other spot on campus.

Next, I talked to two current UK art students, Taylor Blackburn and Makayla Thomas. They spend most of their day at the art building and go to the gallery often for school related art talks, to support their classmates and professors, and just to enjoy or get inspired. And here they are now.

Makayla: I'm Makayla and I'm an art studio major (Thomas).

Taylor: and I'm Taylor, I'm a digital media and design major (Blackburn).

Me: Why do you come to the Bolivar Art Gallery?

Makayla: So I think that the pieces in there offer a lot of variety and you can … uhh … they have different mediums and also you can just see different artist perspectives through the pieces.

Taylor: I'm easily inspired by art around me so by going in there and looking umm … I don't know it's always changing so you never know what your gonna see in there.

Me: What makes the Bolivar Art Gallery unique in comparison to other galleries in the area?

Taylor: Umm … how constantly its changing, so last week when we went in there it was completely different pieces and now this week, they're all new, so its constantly changing and full of new inspiration, and insight, and ideas.

Me: Umm… what feeling do you get when you're in the gallery?

Makayla: So like Taylor said earlier whenever I enter I just feel really inspired by all of the pieces, and it almost is kinda calming and relaxing.

Me: How do you think the art effects the culture of the space?

When I first asked this question Taylor and Makayla were silent. So I gave them some more time to think and then I asked again.

How do you think the art effects the culture of the space?

Makayla: I think that it makes people very inquisitive and brings forth a sense of curiosity within everyone.

Me: In contrast to Jess's interview you can see how the gallery impacts them in a different way. They even talk about how the gallery is not only interesting and enjoyable to look at, but it impacts their art careers because it is a very inspiring place. The curators of the Bolivar Art Gallery put a lot of time and choose carefully who gets into shows and exhibitions. These amazing artists that come from all different cultures and backgrounds really impact the students and what they create. Recently we had a curator display works from Africa and come into the gallery and do an art talk with us. [soundscape from art talk] It was amazing to hear about how bringing African culture to the US galleries through art has not only impacted the Bolivar Art Gallery greatly but also art galleries across the US. They also talked about how the culture is very dynamic and shows many exhibitions across one semester, drawing in more new people every time. I also found it interesting that when I first asked them what they thought about the culture of the space they didn't have an answer. [cricket soundscape] dead silence. So, I gave them time to think about their answer and asked again. They summed it up using the word inquisitive. Which I think is very fitting, because like Taylor and Makayla I also found it hard to sum up the culture of the gallery into one or a few words because it does really mean something different to everyone who goes. But I do agree that it brings wonder and interest into everyone's lives. It gives people the opportunity to come together and wonder together. The art may take some people in different directions than others but either way the Bolivar Art Gallery has a great dynamic, inquisitive, and diverse culture that will change you in some way if you give it a chance. Thank you so much for listening to my podcast. Go get inspired. Thanks again and good-bye.

Works Cited

Blackburn, Taylor. Personal interview. 15 October 2019.

Crickets. *iMovie*. 16 October 2019.

Hallberg, Jessica. Personal interview. 10 October 2019.

Piano Ballad. *iMovie*. 16 October 2019.

Thomas, Makayla. Personal interview. 15 October 2019.

Link to Project

https://wrd.as.uky.edu/engagedcitizen2020

Photo Essays

Hispanic Students at the University of Kentucky

Jennifer Rodriguez

Our fast-paced summer WRD 110 classes challenge students to find stories worth telling within a brief span of time. Jennifer found her story to tell and the time to tell it well, using all original photos and videos to craft a photo essay on Hispanic students' college experience here at the University of Kentucky. Starting from a place of personal investment in the topic, Jennifer goes on to share how new language, new connections, and newly researched understandings of Hispanic students' place in college can help her and the community she's a part of navigate life at UK.

—Emily Handy

Hispanic Students at The University of Kentucky

By: Jennifer Rodriguez

Introduction: Students feeling undervalued on their college campus can have negative affects on them personally or academically. The controversial issue is students of different cultural backgrounds often feel that they're not a part of their university because they don't have that sense of belonging. In an article by Pat Schneider, she quotes Patrick Sims who says "We certainly have a lot of work to do to reach out to all our communities, the native American community, the Latinx community, the African-American community, all the traditionally marginalized groups." Sims is addressing and aware of the issue occurring at The University of UW-Madison and wants to fix it. My personal connection to this is that I belong to the Latinx community at The University of Kentucky. My intention is to reach out to next years incoming freshman students who have experienced a similar situation. I'm writing to anyone who identifies as Hispanic or Latino to shed light on the social equality problem and show that there are on campus resources to aid them through the college process.

Link To Article

Link to Project

https://wrd.as.uky.edu/engagedcitizen2020

Websites

Differing Stories: A Closer Look at the Way Our Gender and Sexual Identity Shapes Our Experiences at U.K.

Ailis Connors, Luis Ettedgui Rivas, Chris
Yarger, Elena Amayrany Perez

In my WRD 110 class, we built toward a collaborative digital story as our final project. Students worked in groups to build websites using Adobe Spark. They were asked to incorporate interviews from the Nunn Center as well as a variety of other primary and secondary sources. Working in this multimodal platform, students combined elements of visual rhetoric and design with written and oral storytelling to create engaging websites for a public audience. Ailis, Luis, Chris, and Elena worked together to create a truly exemplary story: "Differing Stories: A Closer Look at the Way Our Gender and Sexual Identity Shapes Our Experiences at U.K." Drawing on personal stories from several LGBTQ+ folks in Lexington and supplementing these with careful secondary research, the authors honor the individuality, specificity, and variety of lived experiences. At the same time, they manage to bring them together to make a unified digital story. I feel very proud of the maturity and engagement these students demonstrated throughout their collaborative creative process. It resulted in a nuanced and polished product.

—Abby Rudolph

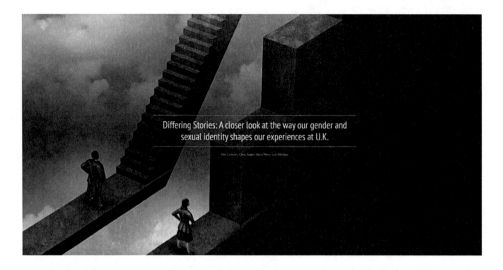

Ahead we will take a look at the past, as well as the present, personal experiences of both students and staff here at The University of Kentucky. Their culminated stories weave a new story, one that expresses just how much our gender and sexual orientation influence our experiences here at U.K..

LinQ Magazine

(Bauer p.1 2015)

This is a Magazine published by the Pride Community Services Organization who were influential activists in the LGBTQ+ community around the city of Lexington Kentucky. The articles within this magazine inform readers of upcoming events and issues within the community, as well as provides motivational words of wisdom to members of the LGBTQ+ community that are experiencing discrimination or hardship.

Link to Project

https://wrd.as.uky.edu/engagedcitizen2020

Public Art in Lexington

Isabel Ibarra, Kiara Rizzuti, Larkyn Rogers

A student's first semester at the University of Kentucky is often disorienting. In addition to being on a jigsaw puzzle of a campus, most students are also adjusting to an unfamiliar town and often a new state as well. Recognizing these trials, Isabel, Kiara, and Larkyn researched and composed a website about public art on campus and in the wider Lexington community for an audience of incoming freshmen for their WRD 110 semester project. Conducting primary research through site observations of galleries and murals, the team documented and reflected on the ways that art changes our relationship to the spaces we inhabit. Through analysis and the authors' personal reflections, the website suggests that the art we encounter tells stories about how we see ourselves, about our place in the world. And by doing so, art also re-creates us as subjects, giving us a chance to understand and feel at home in unfamiliar surroundings. Exploring public art provides these authors a way to adjust to life in the Bluegrass, leading them to recommend their audience "Go out and explore" Lexington's art scene as a way to ease their transition to the UK.

—Craig Crowder

————————————

WRD 110

| HOME | A NEW COMMUNITY | MURALS | GET INVOLVED | MORE |

Public Art in Lexington

WRD 110

| HOME | A NEW COMMUNITY | MURALS | GET INVOLVED | MORE |

Daughter Of Immigrants
By Jessica Sobogal

One mural in particular that caught my eye is done by an artist named Jessica Sabogal. Her art piece is called Daughter Of Immigrants and is located on 167 West Main Street. The reason why I think her artwork got my attention was the colors she chose to stand out dramatically against the building the piece was created on bright yellow against an old brick building. In Daughter Of Immigrants Jessica uses her same pop art tactics to create an effect on the face of the daughter. The second thing that really pulled me into her work is that there is a story behind every single one of her murals. She creates an image of stories she once heard, lived through, struggles and loved. So, specifically in the Daughter of Immigrants, you can imagine that this story can relate to her and it does. She is a first-generation Columbian-American muralist, the goal for her art is to serve as a haven, a tribute, a creative outlet of adoration and exaltation for women with stories often untold. While looking at Jessica's art there is a theme. She's fighting for those who are looked over or pushed around. Her work sticks to women and women of color and different backgrounds, most of her work talks about equality, sex trafficking, education for all, and white power and how it's not given to all.

Link to Project

https://wrd.as.uky.edu/engagedcitizen2020

The Process of Uncovering Racial Injustice

Yogesh Patel, Sharma Ross, Jared Payne

In my WRD 110 class, we built toward a collaborative digital story as our final project. Students worked in groups to build websites using Adobe Spark. They were asked to incorporate interviews from the Nunn Center as well as a variety of other primary and secondary sources. Working in this multimodal platform, students combined elements of visual rhetoric and design with written and oral storytelling to create engaging websites for a public audience. When Sharma, Jared, and Yogesh began their digital story, none of them realized what a journey they would go on. As they researched, they realized that some information they expected to find easily—namely, UK student demographics through the years—was not accessible to them. In fact, it was not accessible at all. Nevertheless, they demonstrated commitment, curiosity, and creative problem-solving. They visited libraries and called administrators. They followed each trail they were led down. The more barriers they faced, the more persistent they became. In the end, they were able to track down some archival documents that helped answer their original research question. "The Process of Uncovering Racial Injustice," is, therefore, part research project, part investigative report.

—Abby Rudolph

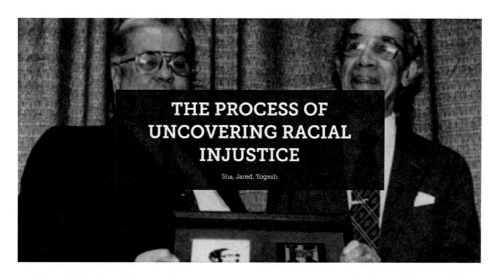

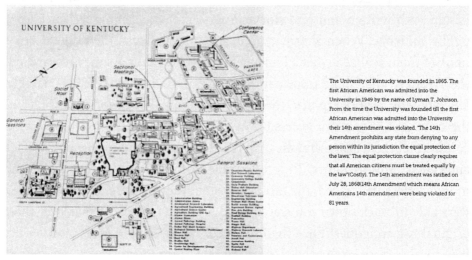

The University of Kentucky was founded in 1865. The first African American was admitted into the University in 1949 by the name of Lyman T. Johnson. From the time the University was founded till the first African American was admitted into the University their 14th amendment was violated. "The 14th Amendment prohibits any state from denying 'to any person within its jurisdiction the equal protection of the laws.' The equal protection clause clearly requires that all American citizens must be treated equally by the law"(Costly). The 14th amendment was ratified on July 28, 1868(14th Amendment) which means African Americans 14th amendment were being violated for 81 years.

Link to Project

https://wrd.as.uky.edu/engagedcitizen2020

Proposal and Annotated Bibliography

The Stigma of the Arts

Makalya Thomas

Although the culminating project in my WRD 110 class is an individual podcast episode, students first submit proposals and annotated bibliographies outlining the research topics they want to explore, which they also transpose in the form of a short oral "pitch" to the class as well. Our broad goal in the course is to be curious but also critical, and we start the semester by unpacking the ways in which other researchers and thinkers have explored topics and issues in their own work. After getting our footing, students embark on a series of tasks that ask them to explore campus and their communities, after which they come away with some topics they propose to learn more about in their investigative podcasts. This is the stage that Makayla Thomas was at when she produced this stellar proposal and annotated bibliography, "The Stigma of the Arts," which seeks to answer a couple of (deceptively) simple questions: why does it seem like the University values the arts much less than it does other disciplines, and what does it mean when lots of other people value it that way too? As Makayla's early research shows, the answer to those questions isn't simple at all, and her proposal charts a broad course for how she plans to pursue it in even more detail in her podcast. An art major herself, Makayla's passion for her subject is matched only by her clear writing and her carefully curated sources. While her final project was outstanding, I was even more impressed with how thoughtful Makayla was here in her proposal at a point in the research process when one's plans are only conjecture. I try to emphasize the importance of scaffolding in my class, of doing big projects one small step at a time—Makayla's work, therefore, provides a great view of what it looks like to value the beginning of a project, not just its end.

—Kendall Sewell

The Stigma of the Arts

When individuals are asked to imagine art, they typically picture pretty paintings on the walls or maybe a famous sculpture of our ancestors, but what would our world be like if there were no art at all? Losing art means more than aesthetic pictures vanishing from our homes. We are constantly surrounded by art and hardly recognize it. The clothes we are wearing, the phone in our pocket, the chair we are sitting in, and even the type of building we are in were all designed by artists. Or what about entertainment? The world would be colorless, soundless, expressionless, and bland. So why is it that art is constantly overlooked by society? As an art student here at the University of Kentucky I have found myself pondering upon this issue quite a bit because of my connection to it. When I am asked what my major is, and I respond with, "Art Studio," most responses are followed by laughter and something along the lines of, "well what can you do with that degree?" Perhaps this is the problem. Art programs are so undermined and swept under the rug that art has lost its appeal due to lack of prioritization. I believe that it is time for people everywhere to be educated on the importance of art and the opportunities that the field holds for those looking for a career.

The particular location that first stemmed this idea was the Fine Arts building here at UK. In comparison to other buildings, it is very run down. I attend class in this building twice a week for my Ballet I class, and there isn't even air conditioning in the dance studio. This makes it a miserable environment for all students. I can't tell you how many times students have had to sit down because of heat exhaustion. If the air conditioning were to be broken in the Don and Cathy Jacobs Science Building, it would be fixed within the next hour. So why are art programs, not only at the University of Kentucky, but other universities as well, not given as many benefits as other programs? Some universities have even gone as far as cutting art programs entirely. This has been a major issue across the United States, especially in Kentucky. When making budget cuts, art programs are the first to go, but art is just as important as other programs. It is almost as if there has been this undefined stigma placed upon the arts that has placed it at the bottom of the academic food chain.

Upon looking further into this topic, I stumbled upon a student-published news article by a girl named Grace Fearon. Grace explores this concept a little more deeply. She explains that "more noticeably than ever, creative subjects are being labeled as 'soft' university subjects, a waste of time to study, and degrees that will almost certainly not lead to employment after graduation. Yet, we seem to have forgotten that, without such studies, we instantly close our minds to the sensitive and intensely human world of creativity" (Fearon). To me, this was an interesting concept. It is almost as if she is suggesting that without art, there is nothing to define us as a human race, and in my opinion, she's right. This is why I have decided to focus my podcast on this issue. This stigma needs to be eliminated for art programs in universities across the country to thrive. If not, I believe that this slow deterioration of these programs will only escalate, leading to the eventual cancellation of art in schools as a whole.

Throughout my podcast, I hope to interview multiple students, both art and non-art majors, as well as faculty and staff members, to gain more insight into varying opinions concerning this subject. I will not mention that I am an art major myself so that they do not feel pressured to give a certain answer in fear of offending me. I will then take the responses I have received to assess the issue further and propose a possible solution. I believe that there is already a lack of knowledge among individuals regarding this specific field, the career opportunities it holds, and its overall contribution to society. This will allow me to investigate this proposed issue first hand, and most importantly, figure out the ultimate question: why?

Annotated Bibliography

Grace Fearon iStudent. "Creativity Is Not Being Seen as a Valuable Skill and This Needs to Change." *The Independent,* Independent Digital News and Media, 17 Dec. 2015, https://www.independent.co.uk/student/istudents/ creativity-is-no-longer-valued-as-a-skill-why-are-we-neglecting-the-arts-a6776686.html.

This source is a student article posted by a news source. This news article, written by Grace Fearon, explores the negative perspective that most people have when viewing art programs at universities. It then gives insight as to why people see the arts in this way. This will be very beneficial to my podcast because it deeply explores the stigma placed on art programs and why these programs are crucially beneficial to society. Although this is a student-written article and not necessarily "fact-based," it is highly credible because of where it is published, and because, for its particular use to me, I need a more "opinion-based" article to incorporate into my podcast.

"Home." *Wallace Foundation,* https://www.wallacefoundation.org/pages/ default.aspx.

The Wallace Foundation is an organization that strives to educate communities on all things art. This site provides multiple resources, especially regarding how to inform people on the arts, as well as the efforts they are already making to do this. This will be helpful to me when I propose my solution to the issue of undereducation in relation to individuals and the arts. This will allow me to propose a solution for my school and community in particular by mimicking things they have done and have been successful with.

Houser, Kyle. *Education and the Fine Arts,* 19 Feb. 2014, https://sites.psu.edu/ richmondcivicissue/2014/02/19/the-benefits-of-fine-arts-education/.

Kyle Houser, a student at Penn State, writes in this article about the benefits of art programs in schools. He mainly focuses on why the arts are just as important as other programs. This is what I particularly admire about this source, especially because it compares the benefits of art to the benefits of other subjects such as math and science, something that the other sources do not. Like the first source, it is written by a student, but the site that published it is extremely credible since it was published by a university. Also, student views are most beneficial to me when it comes to composing my podcast.

"The Value of Arts and Culture to People and Society." *The Value of Arts and Culture to People and Society | Arts Council England,* https://www. artscouncil.org.uk/exploring-value-arts-and-culture/value-arts-and-culture-people-and-society.

On this site provided by the Arts Council of England, there are many pdfs that present valuable statistics as to why the arts are valuable, not only to our emotional/cognitive expression, but to our economy, health and wellbeing, society and education, and culture. This source provides factual evidence to support my claims in my podcast through statistical infographics and other documents. Because this source was published by a credible group that provides useful information that is clearly supported, it will be very beneficial to me and my podcast.

Writers, Staff. "Popular Careers in Art: Turning an Art Degree Into Income." *AccreditedSchoolsOnline.org,* AccreditedSchoolsOnline.org, 23 Oct. 2019, https://www.accreditedschoolsonline.org/art-schools/careers/.

This particular source provides a tremendous amount of information concerning career opportunities in the art field. It not only provides names of potential career options, but descriptions of each job, average annual salaries, and other useful facts. In my podcast, I plan to use examples from this source to show the abundant amount of opportunities this field holds that of which so many people are uninformed about. This source is extremely reliable because it is an accredited source, therefore the organization has been officially authorized.